My United States

Vermont

JENNIFER HACKETT

Children's Press®
An Imprint of Scholastic Inc.

Content Consultant

James Wolfinger, PhD, Associate Dean and Professor
College of Education, DePaul University, Chicago, Illinois

Library of Congress Cataloging-in-Publication Data
Names: Hackett, Jennifer, author.
Title: Vermont / by Jennifer Hackett.
Description: New York, NY : Children's Press, an imprint of Scholastic Inc., 2018. | Series: A true book | Includes
  bibliographical references and index.
Identifiers: LCCN 2017051022| ISBN 9780531235836 (library binding) | ISBN 9780531250969 (pbk.)
Subjects: LCSH: Vermont—Juvenile literature.
Classification: LCC F49.3 .H33 2018 | DDC 974.3—dc23
LC record available at https://lccn.loc.gov/2017051022

Front cover: A boy sledding in Strafford

Back cover: A dairy cow in Rochester

Welcome to Vermont

Find the Truth!

Everything you are about to read is true *except* for one of the sentences on this page.

Which one is **TRUE**?

T or F Vermont was an independent republic before becoming a state.

T or F Vermont is one of the warmest states in the country.

UNITED STATES

Vermont

Find the answers in this book.

Contents

THE **BIG** TRUTH!

Painted turtle

What Represents Vermont?

Maple syrup

Downhill skiing

Mammoth

This Is Vermont!

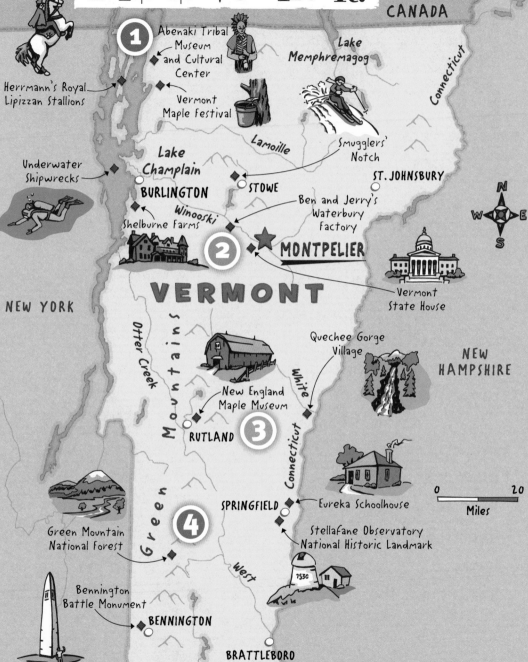

CANADA

1 Abenaki Tribal Museum and Cultural Center

Herrmann's Royal Lipizzan Stallions

Vermont Maple Festival

Lake Memphremagog

Lamoille

Smugglers' Notch

Underwater Shipwrecks

Lake Champlain

BURLINGTON

STOWE

ST. JOHNSBURY

Winooski

Ben and Jerry's Waterbury Factory

Shelburne Farms

2 MONTPELIER

Vermont State House

NEW YORK

VERMONT

Otter Creek

Green Mountains

New England Maple Museum

Quechee Gorge Village

NEW HAMPSHIRE

White

RUTLAND

3

Connecticut

Eureka Schoolhouse

SPRINGFIELD

0 — 20 Miles

Green Mountain National Forest

4

Stellafane Observatory National Historic Landmark

1530

West

Bennington Battle Monument

BENNINGTON

BRATTLEBORO

MASSACHUSETTS

① Abenaki Tribal Museum and Cultural Center

This museum in Swanton honors Vermont's Native American population. It has exhibits on Abenaki life, culture, and art.

MAINE

② Ben and Jerry's Waterbury Factory

The Ben and Jerry's factory in Waterbury is an ice cream lover's dream! It offers guided, 30-minute tours that include plenty of tasting.

③ New England Maple Museum

Vermont's favorite flavor is honored at this museum near Rutland. Exhibits explain how maple syrup is made and explore the tasty topping's history.

④ Green Mountain National Forest

This 400,000-acre (161,874-hectare) forest has more than 2,000 archaeological and historical sites, including Native American sites and colonial farmsteads. It's ablaze with color during the fall, and lucky visitors might even spot a moose!

Vermont is one of five states that have no cities with a population larger than 100,000.

Land and Wildlife

Vermont is a very small state, covering only 9,616 square miles (24,905 square kilometers). However, it has a huge number of forests, mountains, lakeshores, and rivers packed within its borders. It is tucked away in New England in the northeastern United States. The beautiful Green Mountains stretch from north to south across the entire state. Vermont's lowest point, Lake Champlain, makes up part of the state's western border.

Geography

Vermont has six major land regions. In the northwest is the Champlain Valley, a **fertile** farming area and the most developed part of Vermont. South of here are the Taconic Mountains, which produce marble and slate. The Green Mountains run down the center of the state. They're part of the Appalachian Mountains. The state's highest point, Mount Mansfield, is part of this range. It reaches a height of 4,393 feet (1,339 meters).

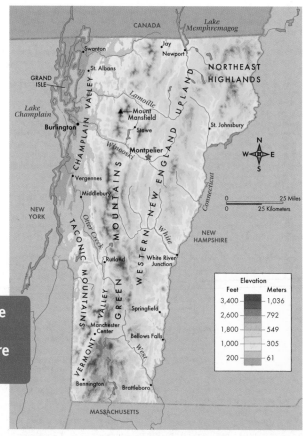

This map shows where the higher (red) and lower (green) areas are in Vermont.

CANADA

Lake Memphremagog

Jay
Newport

Swanton

St. Albans

NORTHEAST
HIGHLANDS

GRAND
ISLE

Lamoille

Lake Champlain

CHAMPLAIN VALLEY

UPLAND

Mount
Mansfield

St. Johnsbury

Burlington

Stowe

Winooski

Montpelier

NEW ENGLAND

Vergennes

Middlebury

Connecticut

N
W—E
S

NEW
YORK

Otter Creek

GREEN MOUNTAINS

TACONIC

WESTERN

0   25 Miles
0   25 Kilometers

NEW
HAMPSHIRE

Rutland

White

White River
Junction

Springfield

VALLEY

Manchester
Center

Bellows Falls

VERMONT

West

Bennington

Brattleboro

MASSACHUSETTS

Elevation	
Feet	Meters
3,400	1,036
2,600	792
1,800	549
1,000	305
200	61

From the shores of Lake Champlain, Vermonters can view the Adirondack Mountains of New York.

Lake Champlain

The large and beautiful Lake Champlain is often called New England's West Coast. Some people call it the sixth Great Lake! It covers 435 square miles (1,127 sq km) and has a maximum depth of 400 feet (122 m). Most of Lake Champlain is in Vermont, but it also stretches into New York and Canada. Dozens of islands dot the lake. According to legend, the lake has a resident sea serpent. It's called Tatoskok by Native Americans and Champ by many of today's Vermonters.

The Northeast Highlands make up the northeastern part of the state. This area is dominated by granite mountains. Nearby is Vermont's second-largest lake, Lake Memphremagog. To the south is the Western New England Upland area, which covers most of eastern Vermont. It has hills, mountains, forests, and streams, as well as rich farmland. Finally, the Vermont Valley in southern Vermont has river valleys along waterways such as Otter Creek and the Walloomsac River.

Located between the Taconic Mountains and the Green Mountains, Emerald Lake State Park is a popular site for boating, fishing, and hiking.

MAXIMUM TEMPERATURE

107°F

MINIMUM TEMPERATURE

-50°F

There are about 50 ski resorts to choose from in Vermont.

Climate

Vermont is the seventh-coldest state in the country! Its annual average temperature is 43 degrees Fahrenheit (6 degrees Celsius). Spring is muddy due to melting snow. Summers are usually mild. In fall, Vermonters start preparing to settle in for the long, cold winter. Temperatures typically stay below freezing for several months, and some areas can receive heavy snowfall.

Tons of Trees

More than three-quarters of Vermont is covered in forests. In the mountains are cone-bearing trees called **conifers**. Varieties found in Vermont include pine, spruce, cedar, and fir trees. The official state tree is the sugar maple. Vermont is famous for delicious maple syrup made from this tree's sap. In fall, the many sugar maple trees put on a beautiful show as their leaves turn bright red and orange.

Ferns are also plentiful throughout Vermont. The curly spiral fiddlehead fern grows in the state's moist, shaded soil. Wildflowers such as daisies and violets are also common.

Maple sap is collected by drilling holes in maple trees and allowing the sap to drip into bags or buckets.

Foxes live in Vermont's forests, mountain areas, and even towns.

Animals

Black bears, bobcats, foxes, minks, woodchucks, and other creatures make the forests of Vermont home. The rivers and lakes are full of trout and other fish. Robins, redwing blackbirds, sparrows, and blue jays take to the skies in the summer. Species such as chickadees, juncos, and nuthatches are present in the winter. On the ground, turkeys, pheasants, and grouse run wild. The rivers, lakes, and ponds are popular with ducks and geese. And white-tailed deer roam across the entire state.

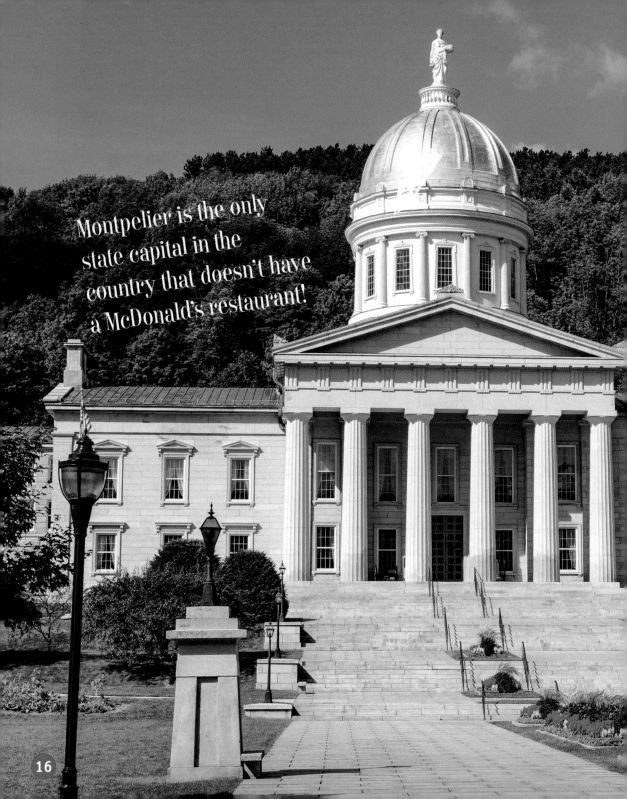

Montpelier is the only state capital in the country that doesn't have a McDonald's restaurant!

CHAPTER 2

Government

The tiny city of Montpelier is Vermont's capital. It is the least populous state capital in the country. Only about 7,500 people live there. But during the day, the population grows to about 21,000 as government workers gather to make laws and carry out other tasks needed for the operation of the state.

Montpelier became Vermont's permanent capital in 1805 due to its convenient central location. The capital was almost moved to Burlington in 1857 after the capitol building burned down. Ultimately, the state stuck with Montpelier.

Branches of Government

Vermont's government is divided into three branches. The governor leads the executive branch, which enforces the state's laws. The General Assembly makes up the state's legislative branch. It has 180 members split between the House of Representatives and the Senate and is responsible for writing laws. The judicial branch is made up of the state's courts. It interprets and upholds these laws.

VERMONT'S STATE GOVERNMENT

EXECUTIVE BRANCH
Carries out state laws

LEGISLATIVE BRANCH
Writes and passes state laws

Governor

General Assembly

Lieutenant Governor | Secretary of State | Attorney General | Treasurer | Auditor

Senate (30 members)

House of Representatives (150 members)

Department heads of:
Agriculture
Corrections
Education
Health
Information and Innovation
Transportation
and many more

JUDICIAL BRANCH
Enforces state laws

Supreme Court

Superior Court

District Court

Family Court

Probate Court

Environmental Court

Judicial Bureau

Citizens gather for a town meeting in Panton.

Government by the People

The first Tuesday in March is Town Meeting Day in Vermont. Across the state, Vermonters meet to elect officials, pass laws, and approve budgets. They also vote on issues important to their communities, like which roads need repairing or how to deal with climate change. On Town Meeting Day, Vermonters take part directly in their government instead of letting their representatives speak for them.

Vermont in the National Government

Each state elects officials to represent it in the U.S. Congress. Like every state, Vermont has two senators. The U.S. House of Representatives relies on a state's population to determine its numbers. Vermont has just one representative in the House.

Every four years, states vote on the next U.S. president. Each state is granted a number of electoral votes based on its number of members of Congress. With two senators and one representative, Vermont has three electoral votes.

2 senators and 1 representative

3 electoral votes

With three electoral votes, Vermont's voice in presidential elections is below average compared to other states.

The People of Vermont

Elected officials in Vermont represent a population with a range of interests, lifestyles, and backgrounds.

Ethnicity (2016 estimates)

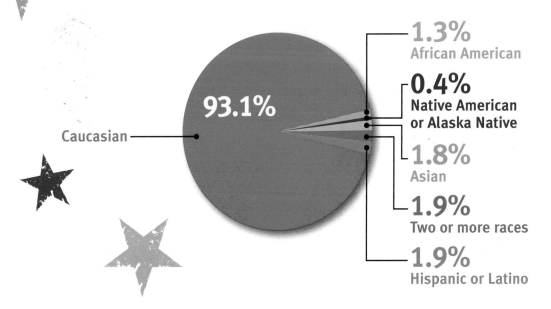

93.1% Caucasian

1.3% African American

0.4% Native American or Alaska Native

1.8% Asian

1.9% Two or more races

1.9% Hispanic or Latino

30.6% have a college degree.

4.3% were born in other countries.

5.4% speak a language other than English at home.

91.8% of the population graduated from high school.

71% own their own homes.

What Represents Vermont?

States choose specific animals, plants, and objects to represent the values and characteristics of the land and its people. Find out why these symbols were chosen to represent Vermont or discover surprising curiosities about them.

Seal

Vermont's state seal shows a pine tree, grain that represents agriculture, and a cow that represents dairy farming. The 14 branches on the tree symbolize the 13 original colonies, with Vermont as the 14th state. The state's motto, "Freedom and Unity," runs along the bottom.

Flag

Vermont's state flag displays the state's coat of arms on a blue field. The coat of arms is a design very similar to the state seal. However, it is more detailed, and it also shows mountains and a deer's head perched on top.

Apple Pie

STATE PIE

According to Vermont state law, a good faith effort should always be made to serve apple pie with a glass of cold milk, a slice of cheddar cheese, or a large scoop of vanilla ice cream.

Painted Turtle

STATE REPTILE

One of the reasons the painted turtle was adopted as the state reptile is because it can withstand cold temperatures like the citizens of Vermont.

Maple

STATE FLAVOR

Vermont produces almost 2 million gallons (7.6 million liters) of maple syrup each year!

Mount Holly Mammoth Tooth and Tusk

STATE FOSSIL

Fossils from this massive animal were discovered in 1848 at Mount Holly. The tooth weighs nearly 8 pounds (4 kilograms), and the tusk is 80 inches (2 m) long!

Milk

STATE BEVERAGE

There are about 1,000 dairy farms in Vermont. They produce milk from cattle, sheep, and goats.

Apple

STATE FRUIT

About 150 different kinds of apples grow in Vermont's **orchards**.

Caribou were once an important food source for Vermont's Native Americans.

CHAPTER 3

History

The French explorer Samuel de Champlain first saw Vermont in 1609. He followed waterways from Canada to Lake Champlain, which was named for him. The mountain peaks in the distance looked green because of their dense tree cover. As a result, the region came to be known as *Verd Mont*. These are the French words for "green mountain." They were eventually combined to become the name Vermont.

Native Americans

Native Americans first arrived in Vermont about 13,000 years ago. By about 1000 BCE, the Abenaki people lived in northern New England and across all of Vermont. They joined with other native groups in the Wabanaki Confederacy. This helped them defend against raids by the Iroquois of upstate New York. The Mohican and Pennacook also lived in what is now Vermont.

This map shows some of the major tribes that lived in what is now Vermont before Europeans came.

The Abenaki people made their homes along riverbanks in groups averaging about 50 to 100 people. They didn't have a central leader. Instead, family groups governed themselves. Each group had a spiritual leader called a sachem. Several groups might band together to fight wars, led by a single sachem. All adults took part in discussions about important matters relating to war and peace.

Vermont's Native Americans taught European settlers how to make maple syrup.

Explorers From Abroad

The first European explorers in Vermont were French. They came from the **colony** of New France, which was in present-day Canada. Although French settlers were the first to explore Vermont, the first permanent settlement in Vermont was established by the British in 1724. Many more British settlers arrived soon after this. They trapped animals for fur and traded with French settlers and Native Americans.

This map shows the route Samuel de Champlain took as he explored what is now Vermont.

Future U.S. president George Washington (on horseback) served as a British military officer during the French and Indian War.

With British settlers taking over more and more of Vermont, France began to fear that it would lose control of the region. The rivalry between France and Britain led to the French and Indian War (1754–1763). During this conflict, French and British settlers battled each other for control of North America. Each side was aided by different Native American groups. Upon France's defeat in 1763, Vermont officially became British **territory**.

From Independence to Statehood

Vermont helped the American colonies fight the British in the Revolutionary War (1775–1783), but it was not an official colony itself. Both New York and New Hampshire tried to claim its land as their own. In 1777, Vermont declared itself the **Republic** of New Connecticut, controlled by neither Great Britain nor the American colonies. After the war, it remained an independent republic.

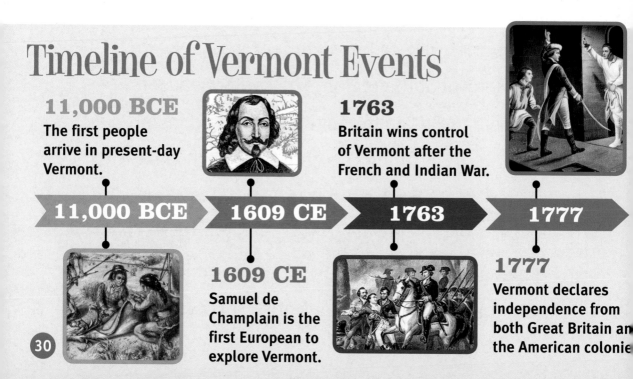

Timeline of Vermont Events

11,000 BCE
The first people arrive in present-day Vermont.

1763
Britain wins control of Vermont after the French and Indian War.

11,000 BCE ▸ **1609 CE** ▸ **1763** ▸ **1777**

1609 CE
Samuel de Champlain is the first European to explore Vermont.

1777
Vermont declares independence from both Great Britain and the American colonies

For 14 years, Vermont argued with New York over land rights. Finally, in 1790, Vermont paid New York $30,000 to give up its claims on the region. This enabled it to become the 14th state on March 4, 1791. Slavery had long been outlawed in Vermont. When the Civil War (1861–1865) broke out, 34,000 Vermonters fought for the Union. Among them were about 150 African Americans who had come to Vermont as escaped or freed slaves.

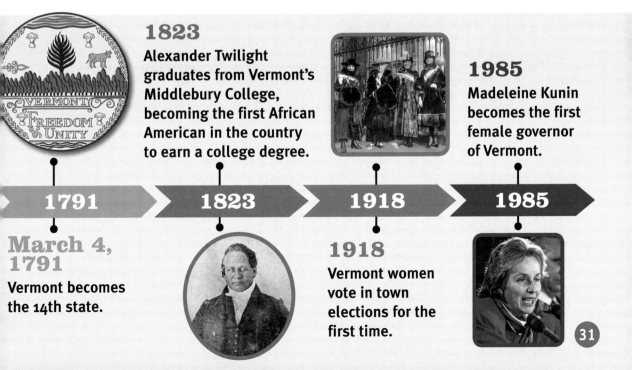

1823
Alexander Twilight graduates from Vermont's Middlebury College, becoming the first African American in the country to earn a college degree.

1985
Madeleine Kunin becomes the first female governor of Vermont.

1791 **1823** **1918** **1985**

March 4, 1791
Vermont becomes the 14th state.

1918
Vermont women vote in town elections for the first time.

Loggers such as the one shown here in September 1903 relied on horses to help drag heavy trees out of Vermont's forests.

Modern Vermont

After the Civil War ended, Vermont's **industries** prospered. They included dairy farming, logging, and machine manufacturing. In the 1900s, Vermont's natural beauty and the increased ease of traveling made it a popular place to vacation. Tourism increased after the end of World War II (1939–1945). Today, the state remains a popular vacation destination.

Although he was born in Connecticut in 1738, Ethan Allen helped shape Vermont's early history. He bought land in Vermont in the late 1760s. When New York was awarded control of the territory by Great Britain, Allen's land was taken away. He led an armed force called the Green Mountain Boys against New York settlers to keep his land. He later led the same force against the British-held Fort Ticonderoga in 1775, successfully taking control of it. Allen's fighting spirit and political involvement helped shape Vermont's independence and political character for decades.

Ethan Allen (center) commands the surrender of the British military leader during the capture of Fort Ticonderoga.

Built in 1906, the *Ticonderoga* transported passengers around Vermont and New York until 1953.

The 220-foot (67 m) steamboat *Ticonderoga* is displayed outside the Shelburne Museum.

Culture

Vermont's beautiful **rural** scenery has inspired countless painters over the years. The Shelburne Museum displays many of their landscapes. Traditional crafts such as woodcarving, quilting, and granite carving thrive throughout the state. Abenakis preserve centuries-old basket-weaving traditions, using sweetgrass and ash bark to make stunning creations. The poet Robert Frost moved to Vermont in 1920, and *Bridge to Terabithia* author Katherine Paterson calls the state home.

Millions of people visit Vermont each winter to ski and snowboard on the state's snowy mountains.

Sports and Recreation

Vermont has no major professional sports teams. However, schools such as the University of Vermont and Middlebury College have popular lacrosse, soccer, hockey, and skiing teams.

When it comes to skiing, few places can beat Vermont. Olympic hopefuls often train on Vermont's snowy slopes. Vermonters have taken home Olympic medals in downhill skiing, cross-country skiing, and snowboarding.

The Penguin Plunge is a charity event that raises money for athletes with intellectual disabilities.

Festivals

Vermont's music, food, nature, and art are celebrated at festivals held all year. The Marlboro Music Festival celebrates classical music, with performances from master musicians and their students. Fall festivals such as the Cabot Apple Pie Festival celebrate Vermont's beautiful trees and the fruit they produce. The North Bennington Winter Festival shows off ice sculptures and hosts a Penguin Plunge into freezing water. And, of course, the Vermont Maple Festival in Saint Albans celebrates the state's signature syrup.

A worker oversees the production of pepper jack cheese at the Cabot Creamery cheese factory.

Work

Most Vermonters work in jobs that provide a service to others. These include teaching, providing health care, and working in retail. The tourism industry also has many jobs, from running hotels to giving tours. Vermonters also make many things, including ice cream at Ben and Jerry's, cheese at Cabot Creamery, and teddy bears at the Vermont Teddy Bear Company. The state's largest individual employer is the University of Vermont.

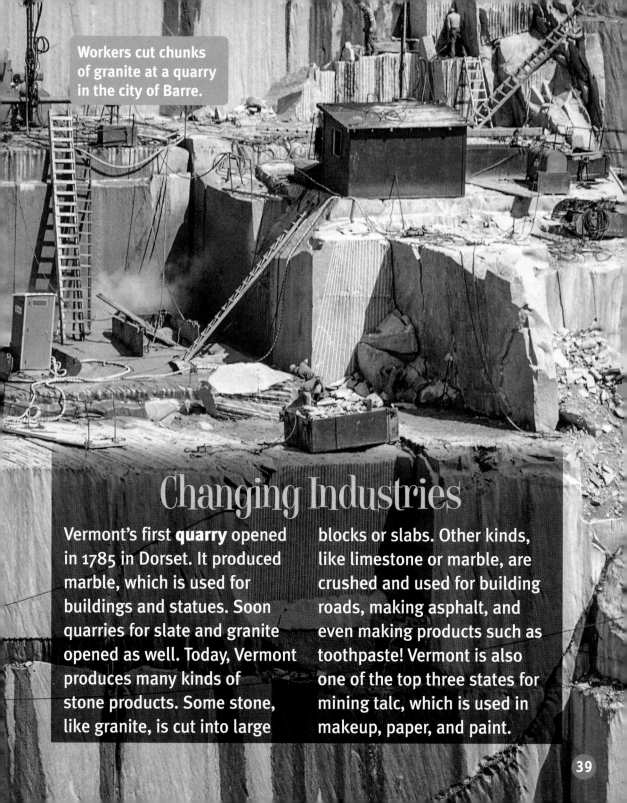

Workers cut chunks of granite at a quarry in the city of Barre.

Changing Industries

Vermont's first **quarry** opened in 1785 in Dorset. It produced marble, which is used for buildings and statues. Soon quarries for slate and granite opened as well. Today, Vermont produces many kinds of stone products. Some stone, like granite, is cut into large blocks or slabs. Other kinds, like limestone or marble, are crushed and used for building roads, making asphalt, and even making products such as toothpaste! Vermont is also one of the top three states for mining talc, which is used in makeup, paper, and paint.

Maple and More

From Lake Champlain Chocolates to Ben and Jerry's ice cream, Vermont is known for fantastic sweets. The state also has dairy farms where delicious sharp cheddar cheese is made. But Vermont's most famous treat is maple syrup. It produces more of this syrup than any other state.

Maple Pie

Ask an adult to help you!

This unique pie features Vermont's most famous flavor.

Ingredients
1 $1/2$ cups heavy cream
$3/4$ cup all-purpose flour
1 $1/2$ cups pure Vermont maple syrup
2 tablespoons butter
$1/4$ teaspoon black pepper
1 9-inch unbaked pie shell

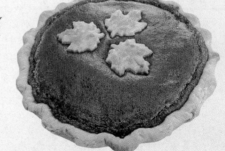

Directions
In a saucepan, whisk the cream and flour together until smooth. Add the maple syrup, butter, and pepper. Stir while cooking over medium heat for 10 minutes, or until thickened. Pour the filling into the pie shell. Bake at 350° F for 20 to 30 minutes. Cool on a rack. Once the pie reaches room temperature, put it in the refrigerator to cool.

A mountain biker gets a close look at some cows as he passes through a pasture near Fayston.

A Surprising State

Vermont is a state full of surprises. It is fiercely independent but also welcoming to new people. It keeps traditions like basket weaving and quilting alive while embracing new activities like snowboarding and music festivals. And it does not lack in delicious treats! It's a beautiful place to live or visit, especially for people who love spending time in nature. ★

Famous People

Alexander Twilight

(1795–1857) was the first African American to earn a college degree and also the first African American elected to state-level public office in the United States. He was from Corinth.

John Deere

(1804–1886) invented the steel plow in 1837 and also founded Deere & Company, which is now one of the world's largest makers of farm equipment. He was born in Rutland.

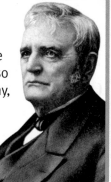

Elisha Otis

(1811–1861) invented the safety elevator, which won't fall if its cables break. Most elevators today bear his name. He was a native of Halifax.

Martin Henry Freeman

(1826–1889) became the first African American president of a U.S. college in 1856. He was born in Rutland.

Annette Parmelee

(1865–1924) fought for women's rights, including the right to vote. She earned the nickname **Suffragette** Hornet for her activism. She was from Enosburg.

Calvin Coolidge

(1872–1933) was the 30th president of the United States. He was from Plymouth.

Robert Frost

(1874–1963) was a famous poet who wrote about rural life. He taught at Middlebury College.

Dorothy Thompson

(1893–1961) was a journalist in the 1930s and 1940s who worked to raise awareness of the threat Adolf Hitler posed in the years before World War II. She lived in Barnard.

Consuelo N. Bailey

(1899–1976) was the first woman admitted to practice law before the U.S. Supreme Court. She became the nation's first female lieutenant governor when she won the Vermont election in 1954.

Katherine Paterson

(1932–) is an author who has won many awards and even had her book *Bridge to Terabithia* made into a movie in 2007. She lives in Barre.

Bernie Sanders

(1941–) has represented Vermont in both the U.S. House of Representatives and the U.S. Senate. He's the longest-serving independent (neither Democrat nor Republican) member of Congress in U.S. history! Sanders was also a leading candidate for U.S. president in 2016.

Bill Koch

(1955–) became the first American to win an Olympic medal in cross-country skiing in 1976. He is from Brattleboro.

Did You Know That...

Vermont was the first state to join the Union that wasn't one of the original 13 colonies. It was also the first state to outlaw slavery and allow same-sex civil unions.

There is one dairy cow for every 2.6 people in Vermont. That's the nation's highest ratio of dairy cows to people.

It takes 40 gallons (151 L) of maple sap to produce a single gallon of maple syrup.

The von Trapp family, which inspired the musical *The Sound of Music*, moved to Stowe, Vermont, in 1942. Their descendants still run a ski lodge.

More than 20 cities across the United States—including New York, Nashville, Las Vegas, and Washington, D.C.—have greater populations than the entire state of Vermont.

Vermont has only one telephone area code: 802.

Zebra mussels live in colonies of up to 65,000 mussels per 1 square foot (0.09 sq m). This **invasive species** was accidentally transported to Lake Champlain. The state is working on how to control this pesky population.

Did you find the truth?

(T) Vermont was an independent republic before becoming a state.

(F) Vermont is one of the warmest states in the country.

Resources

Books

Bailer, Darice. *What's Great About Vermont?* Minneapolis: Lerner Publications, 2016.

Czech, Jan M. *Vermont.* New York: Children's Press, 2009.

Heinrichs, Ann. *Vermont.* New York: Children's Press, 2014.

Rozett, Louise (ed.). *Fast Facts About the 50 States: Plus Puerto Rico and Washington, D.C.* New York: Children's Press, 2010.

Visit this Scholastic website for more information on Vermont:

 www.factsfornow.scholastic.com
Enter the keyword **Vermont**

Important Words

colony (KAH-luh-nee) a territory that has been settled by people from another country and is controlled by that country

conifers (KAH-nuh-furz) evergreen trees that produce their seeds in cones

fertile (FUR-tuhl) land that is good for growing crops and plants

industries (IN-duh-streez) single branches of business or trade

invasive species (in-VAY-siv SPEE-sheez) a plant or animal species that is introduced to an area where it is not native, changing the environment's natural balance

orchards (OR-churdz) areas of land where fruit or nut trees are grown

quarry (KWOR-ee) a place where stone, slate, or sand is dug from the ground

republic (rih-PUHB-lik) a form of government in which the people have the power to elect representatives who manage the government

rural (ROOR-uhl) of or having to do with the countryside, country life, or farming

suffragette (suf-ruh-JET) a woman who fights for voting rights

territory (TER-ih-tor-ee) an area connected with or owned by a country that is outside the country's main borders

Index

Page numbers in **bold** indicate illustrations.

About the Author

Jennifer Hackett studied physics and history at the College of William and Mary. But before that, she was born in Burlington, Vermont! She has written about space exploration, climate change, and cool technology, but loves any excuse to talk about history and her beautiful childhood home. She currently works as Scholastic MATH's associate editor. Her favorite Ben and Jerry's flavor? It's a tie between Phish Food and Coffee, Coffee BuzzBuzzBuzz.